# The Pupil's Day

## Ann Cook and Herb Mack

28-90

Citation Press, New York 1971

© Schools Council Publications 1971.

ISBN 590-09517-X

Library of Congress Catalog Card Number 75-168880

## The Authors

**Ann Cook** and **Herb Mack** are the co-directors of the Community Resources Institute of the City University of New York. The Institute is concerned largely with in-service and pre-service training of teachers and school administrators and the development of materials for classroom use. Miss Cook and Mr Mack have taught in both American and English schools, and have written on educational developments in both countries.

This book is published simultaneously in Great Britain, Canada and other countries of the British Commonwealth by Macmillan Education Ltd and in the United States by Citation Press, Library and Trade Division Scholastic Magazines, Inc.

Designer Richard Hollis

Printed in the U.S.A.

# Preface

The purpose of the Anglo-American Primary Education Project is to provide descriptions of the way that British primary schools work. They are published in this series of booklets under the general title of *Informal Schools in Britain Today* and they have been written for American and British educators and teachers-in-training as well as for the general public.

The authors are either practitioners or expert observers of British primary education and, in most cases, they document the work of the schools through detailed case examples; where it is relevant, implications are stated and conclusions drawn. It is not the intention to provide theoretical discussions or prescriptive manuals to informal education, but rather to present accounts from which deductions and generalizations can be made. In so doing, these booklets draw on the experience of that large minority of primary schools that have adopted informal methods.

It is hoped that the booklets will help educators who are looking for examples to substantiate change in particular schools and also those who are concerned, as teachers, educators or administrators, with the wider implications of the education of young children. For students who plan to become teachers these accounts of what happens in the classrooms of British primary schools provide ample material for discussion as well as helpful insights into the practice of teaching.

The series has been prepared under the aegis of the Schools Council in England with the support of the Ford Foundation in the United States. Planning was assisted by a small Anglo-American advisory group whose members are listed on page 4. The views expressed are however personal to each author.

**British Directorate**

**Geoffrey Cockerill, Project Chairman**/Joint Secretary, Schools Council for Curriculum and Examinations, London.

**John Blackie**/Formerly Chief Inspector, Primary Education, Department of Education and Science, London.

**Molly Brearley**/Formerly Principal, Froebel Institute College of Education, London.

**Maurice Kogan, Project Co-ordinator**/Professor of Government and Social Administration, School of Social Sciences, Brunel University, Uxbridge, Middlesex.

**American Participants**

**J. Myron Atkin**/Dean, School of Education, University of Illinois, Urbana, Illinois.

**Ann Cook**/Co-director, Community Resources Institute, 270 W.96th Street, New York.

**Joseph Featherstone**/Writer; Lecturer, John Fitzgerald Kennedy School of Government, Institute of Politics, Harvard University, Cambridge, Massachusetts.

**Professor David Hawkins**/Director, Mountain View Center for Environmental Education, University of Colorado, Boulder, Colorado.

**Herb Mack**/Co-director, Community Resources Institute, 270 W.96th Street, New York.

**Marjorie Martus**/Program Officer, The Ford Foundation, New York, NY.

**Casey Murrow**/Teacher, Wilmington Elementary School, Wilmington, Vermont.

**Liza Murrow**/Antioch-Putney Graduate School of Education, Putney, Vermont.

**Mary Lela Sherburne**/Director, Pilot Communities Project, Education Development Center, Newton, Mass.

The photographic studies which follow show, in sequence, the experiences of five primary pupils during a typical day in school.

In selecting the children, we were guided by the judgment of the head who, in consultation with the class teacher, chose the particular child for study.

The five represent particular types of children found in a typical classroom: the newcomer who 'flits' from area to area and the child who has settled in after an initial period of wandering; the child whose learning style touches many areas of interest and the child who is most comfortable with a concentrated focus; the child who is especially motivated by the creative arts and the one who is attracted to writing and mathematics. Additionally, those children photographed represent a group of mixed ages and abilities, both boys and girls, from varying social backgrounds.

# 1 Henry

The child in this sequence had been in school only three weeks. He is constantly exploring, testing and trying to come to terms with the school environment. He is typical of those children who need a good deal of time to adjust to the environment, to establish relationships with other children and to begin to learn to concentrate.

then in the reading corner.

Next he becomes fascinated by the class hamster

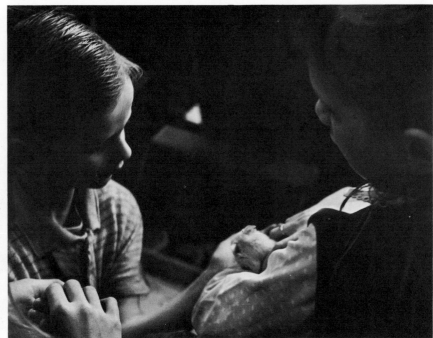

and gets food to feed the pet.

He is prevented by the teacher from overfeeding the pet.

The teacher talks about another activity available in the science corner, observing the tadpoles.

The teacher watches what Henry does and discusses the tadpoles.

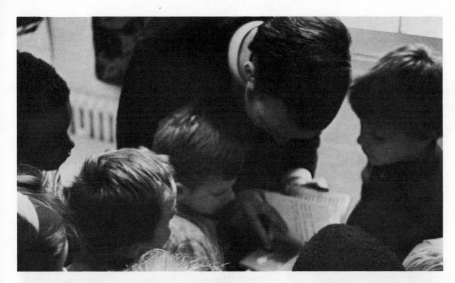

Henry finds a book
about the creatures
and is joined
by other
interested children.

Taking the
opportunity to explore
different parts of
the science area,
the teacher discusses
plants which have been
planted by others
in the class.

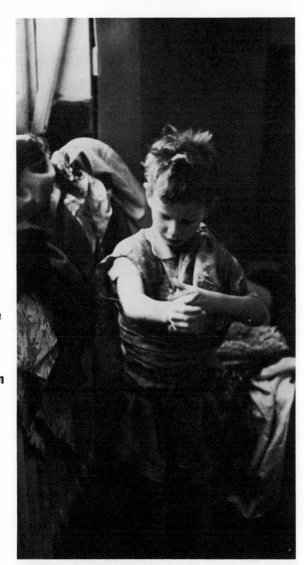

Henry's attention wanders, and he
goes to the dressing-up clothes.
Once again he is alone.

Dressed up, he moves through the school, into the corridor, and into the head's room. The head discusses his activities with him.

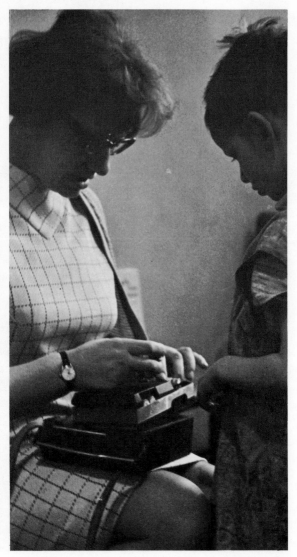

He is fascinated by her tape recorder, and the two record a conversation, listen to it, and discuss Henry's morning.

While wandering back towards his class, he explores the school — stopping at a classroom door to watch and listen.

He is found by the teacher, and taken upstairs for the annual class photo.

11

**Returning to the classroom,
Henry briefly joins in painting, makes quite a mess**

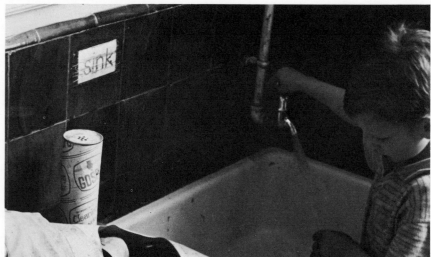

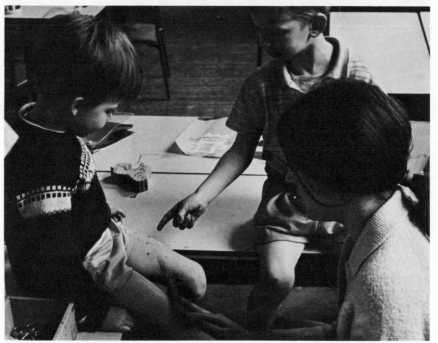

**and is helped
to clean up
by a teacher in
the adjoining room.**

**Pausing for a bottle of milk,**

**Henry and his special friend go to the block area**

**and construct 'guns'.**    **The teacher discusses their construction**    **and plays the 'bad guy'.**

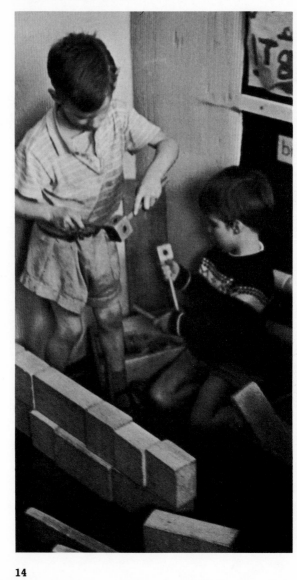

Those children interested are invited to watch
a special educational broadcast. Henry goes along,
but ignores the programme.

Caught by the music, he joins the others.

As the children
return to the
classroom activity,
Henry explores
the playground.

Moving a bookshelf,

he goes to the doll's house,
where an energetic push
topples it over.

As he peeps around the side,
the teacher intervenes to salvage the structure.

The group is drawn together, discusses words,
and listens to a story

while Henry goes to
the book corner
for a look.

Lunch time,
the first sustained
encounter demanding
his participation,
results in friction —
quickly handled
by the teacher.

Henry's afternoon
begins, as he
once again appears
in the head's room.

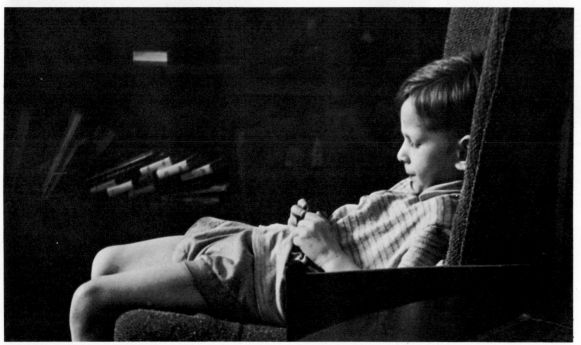

He uses the dial on her telephone,

**plays with the mechanical desk calendar**

**and finally,
on her return,
listens to a story**

**and explores
the 'talking page'.**

Joining the group
outside,

he finds it
somewhat difficult
to follow the rules
of an organized game.

His day, an extremely full one,
comes to an end.

# 2 Nicki

Nicki is a six-year-old boy who took some time to adjust to the classroom environment. In many respects he was similar to Henry (of the first sequence), lacking concentration and something of a loner. Now in his second year of school, he has settled in, and is capable of spending long periods of time engaged in one activity.

**and a discussion about the choice of activities.**

**and cuts it.**

**Nicki chooses cooking, and works out how to divide the butter**

**He measures it into thirds
(a piece for each child involved)**

**and distributes it around.**

**He prepares the scale for weighing**

**and watches the sugar being poured with the teacher's guidance.**

**A more experienced child measures the first tablespoon of milk,**

followed by Nicki, who pours it into his own bowl.

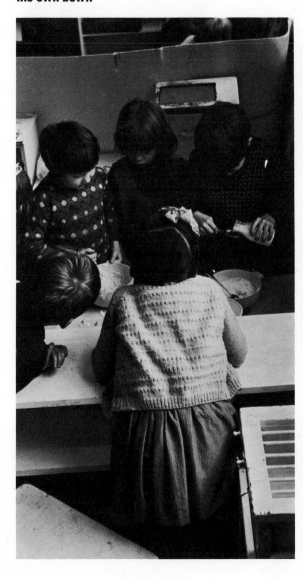

The mixing done, he drops the batter into the tin,

pauses to watch his friend,

**and samples the product.**

The teacher shuts the troublesome oven door, while the children

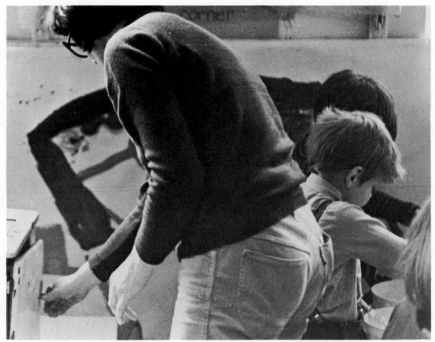

begin the washing up.

The baking finished, he and his friends, having calculated the costs and yield, sell cakes to the headmistress.

Pausing after a busy hour and a quarter, Nicki chats with friends,

then asks the teacher to find him his writing book.

**She helps him settle in.**

**Illustrating and writing a story on football,**

**he pauses, stumped for a word he needs,**

**and takes his word book to the teacher for help.**

**The teacher supplies the word**

and Nicki carries on
with his writing.

Finished, he takes it
to show the teacher,

who discusses
the story with him

**and shares it with the others.**

**She reads another child's story before the children break for lunch.**

**The afternoon begins with a search for a particular book displayed in the corridor book rack.**

**A teacher listens to him read, followed by**

activity in the water area,
where he constructs a toy that will float.

The day ends with
a concentrated effort at
clearing up, in the area
where he worked

and the room at large.

# 3 Ami

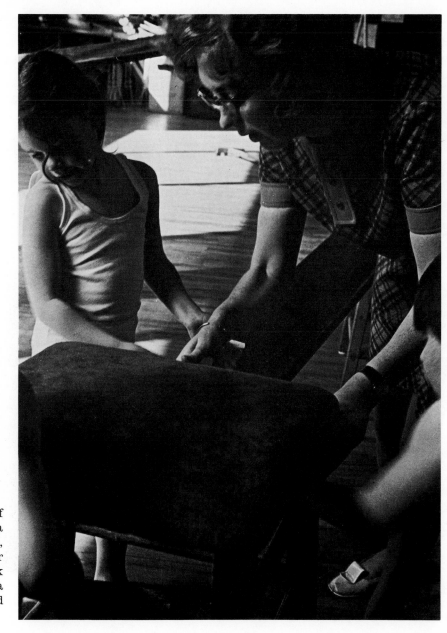

The day begins
with the teacher
and selected children
setting up one of
the few scheduled
activities of the day:
PE (physical education).
Because the activity
requires use of
common space,
groups are assigned
specific times.

Ami, one of the older five-year-olds in a class of
first-year children, is successfully involved in a
variety of classroom activities. She reads well,
after an initial anxiety about the alphabet. Her
sewing activities have led to considerable work
in mathematics. She seems able to create a
calm, self-contained private world, separated
from the classroom activity surrounding her.

To increase awareness of body and space,
children are set problems, such as —
'move within a small area'.

Returning to the classroom, children choose activities.
Individual folders, dictionaries, pencils and writing and maths books
are readily accessible.

Books with words requested by the individual child help story writing, and illustration develops creative expression.
The teacher moves about, raises questions and offers support.

A child may be asked to complete projects begun on previous occasions.
Classroom areas carefully stocked and neatly arranged encourage follow-through.

Activities such as sewing are regarded as valuable learning experiences.

At times the entire class may be gathered together for a common experience, and use of the local environment is frequent. Although a large group may participate, the desire to follow through may be generated in only a few of the children.

Reading becomes an interest of natural involvement,

fostered by the classroom aide, who listens and assists.

The teacher is always available for
individual help as questions arise —
an occasion for others to learn as well.

A class teacher with a special interest or skill
may be available to the children throughout the school,
both informally and on a scheduled basis.

A music club brings together those children who are particularly keen to do concentrated work in composition, rhythm and listening.

In some classes, the day ends with all the children discussing the day's experiences, showing things they've made, or listening to a record the teacher has selected.

# 4 Chris

Chris is one of the older children in the infant school. He tends to become involved in one particular activity for extended periods of time. At the time these pictures were taken, he was concentrating almost exclusively on mathematics, and was frequently joined by a friend who had the same interest. Prior to the work in mathematics, Chris had spent several months focusing on reading and writing, to the exclusion of almost everything else; before that it was art and creative work. Chris would also volunteer for participation in such group activities as movement. He seems to work in relatively short, intensive spurts, alternating with longer periods of relaxation combining investigation and conversation.

As deputy head, she takes the school assembly
and discusses the morning's activities with Chris, and other children in her class, when the assembly breaks up.

Chris returns to his room, and settles into the mathematics area,
where he has spent a great deal of his time in recent weeks.

As the teacher helps the children begin their work,
Chris and a friend relax and talk.

They begin to record their activities,
while the teacher helps another child.

Informal chat continues

43

until she turns her attention to the two boys. Picking up from their previous day's work, she asks questions.

The boys spend a considerable amount of time working through the problems,

**using different number bases,**

**and recording their work.**

Given the opportunity to volunteer for movement,
Chris moves into the hall.

**Half an hour later, he is back in the classroom, working again in the mathematics area.**

**Morning coffee is served to the teacher**

as she works with the children.

After looking over their notebooks she sets new problems for the two boys.

She moves to another group of children,

while Chris and friend carry on their work.

The morning comes to an end with physical education, taken by the class teacher in the large hall.

**The children work through various physical movements**

**aimed at improving co-ordination.**

**The afternoon work becomes more individualized, as Chris continues his concentration on mathematics.**

**Work with the number board**

is supported by the teacher,

as others carry on their work.

Having spent almost the entire day on mathematics work,
Chris helps to clear up

and does a thorough job of straightening the various classroom areas

while the group joins together for a class tradition: story telling by the children and the teacher.

**Finally satisfied with the condition of the room, he joins the others.**

# 5 Gillian

Children arrive slowly
and choose a
starting activity.
A weekend visit to
the fairground
becomes the focal point
of a morning's work.
The written
description

Gillian is a seven-year-old who has spent three years with her teacher. She is described as an average child in areas such as reading and mathematics, but as talented in music and inventive in art. Gillian tends to seek the companionship of other children, and to become stimulated by her contact with them.

may be followed by preparation for, and involvement in, the visual record.

**Friends join in.**

The activity is allowed to continue,
even while others take physical education in the hall.

The 'caterpillar' ride becomes transformed
into a large, colourful work of art.

Selecting a book is routine but may be helped by the teacher's presence.

Activity flows from one interaction to another, and one child's finished product becomes the catalyst for another's involvement.

The friendly atmosphere of the classroom provides ample opportunity for relaxation and mixing.

A morning's activity is discussed and enjoyed by all.

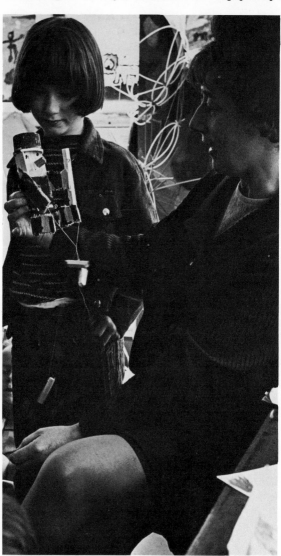

A lunch-hour play-time involves three children in long-term preparation for the school festival

and is discussed with the teacher, whose lunch time, too, is spent in and out of the classroom.

Instruments are available for the particularly keen.

The class teacher becomes
the temporary music 'specialist',
as interest spreads.

Activity flows into common areas.
Here manipulative materials provide mathematical experience.

As end-of-the-day stories are presided over
by a part-time teacher,

and clearing-up activities progress,
the teacher herself remains available for the last bit of help.

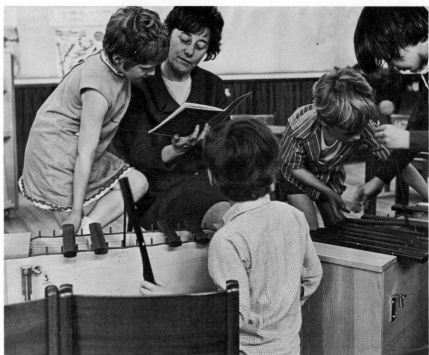

64

## DATE DUE

| | | | |
|---|---|---|---|
| Sept 12, 1980 | | | |
| MAR 1 7 1982 | | | |
| | | | |
| | | | |
| | | | |
| | | | |
| | | | |
| | | | |
| | | | |
| | | | |
| | | | |
| | | | |
| | | | |
| | | | |
| | | | |
| | | | |
| | | | |